TOOLS OF THE TRADE

SandCastle
Tools of the Trade

SCREWDRIVERS

ANDERS HANSON

Consulting Editor, Diane Craig, M.A./Reading Specialist

ABDO
Publishing Company

Published by ABDO Publishing Company, 8000 West 78th Street, Edina, Minnesota 55439.

Copyright © 2010 by Abdo Consulting Group, Inc. International copyrights reserved in all countries.

Printed in the United States.

Editor: Pam Price
Content Developer: Nancy Tuminelly
Cover and Interior Design and Production: Mighty Media
Photo Credits: Shutterstock

Library of Congress Cataloging-in-Publication Data
Hanson, Anders, 1980-
   Screwdrivers / Anders Hanson.
       p. cm. -- (Tools of the trade)
   ISBN 978-1-60453-585-3
   1. Screwdrivers--Juvenile literature. I. Title.

TJ1201.S34H35 2009
621.9'72--dc22

                                        2008055715

SandCastle™ Level: Fluent

SandCastle™ books are created by a team of professional educators, reading specialists, and content developers around five essential components—phonemic awareness, phonics, vocabulary, text comprehension, and fluency—to assist young readers as they develop reading skills and strategies and increase their general knowledge. All books are written, reviewed, and leveled for guided reading, early reading intervention, and Accelerated Reader® programs for use in shared, guided, and independent reading and writing activities to support a balanced approach to literacy instruction. The SandCastle™ series has four levels that correspond to early literacy development. The levels are provided to help teachers and parents select appropriate books for young readers.

Emerging Readers
(no flags)

Beginning Readers
(1 flag)

Transitional Readers
(2 flags)

Fluent Readers
(3 flags)

SandCastle™ would like to hear from you. Please send us your comments and suggestions.

sandcastle@abdopublishing.com

CONTENTS

slotted screwdriver

WHAT IS A SCREWDRIVER?

screw   screwdriver

A screwdriver is a tool that **drives** and removes screws. There are many types of screws and screwdrivers. Each type of screwdriver is made to turn a certain type of screw.

HISTORY

Screwdrivers have existed for about 700 years. The first screwdrivers were **slotted**. They had flat blades that could turn slotted screws. Slotted screwdrivers and screws are still used today.

modern slotted screw

old slotted screwdriver

In the 1930s, an American named Henry Phillips invented the Phillips screwdriver and screws.

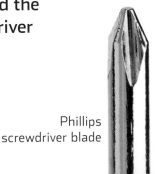

Phillips screwdriver blade

Phillips screws

SLOTTED
SCREWDRIVER

Slotted screwdrivers are made to turn slotted screws.

different types and sizes of slotted screws

blade   shank

The screwdriver blade fits into the slot on the screw head.

different sizes
of slotted
screwdrivers

handle

Slotted screwdrivers have a flat blade.

It takes two hands to **drive** a slotted screw. One hand holds the screw in place while the other turns the screwdriver.

This electrical outlet has **slotted** screws. They can be turned with a slotted screwdriver.

This cable is secured with screws. Henry uses a **slotted** screwdriver to tighten the screws.

PHILLIPS SCREWDRIVER

Phillips screwdrivers can only turn Phillips screws. Phillips screws come in many types and sizes.

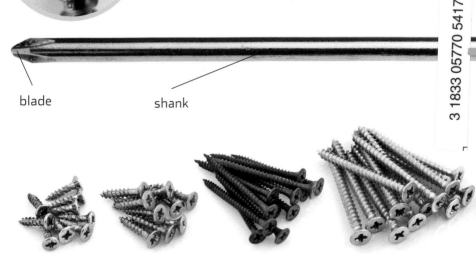

3 1833 05770 5417

blade

shank

different sizes and types of Phillips screws

A Phillips screwdriver has an X-shaped blade tip.

The X shape creates more **friction** between the screwdriver and the screw. This friction makes it easier to turn the screw.

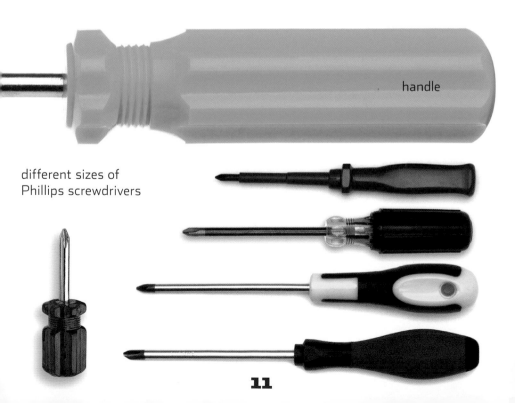

handle

different sizes of Phillips screwdrivers

Gary is fixing a stool. He uses a Phillips screwdriver to **attach** a stool leg.

Peter is **repairing** a computer part.
He is using a Phillips screwdriver.

SCREW GUN

Some screw guns use strips of screws. The strip of screws feeds into the nose of the screw gun.

nose

strip of screws

1-1/4

A screw gun will not operate unless the nose is pressed against something.

screw guard

Screw guns **drive** a lot of screws quickly and easily.

trigger

handle

DS200-AC

A screw gun can drive a new screw about every two seconds.

Candice is **installing** drywall in a new house. She uses a screw gun to **fasten** the drywall.

Megan is building a desk. She is using a screw gun to **drive** screws.

HEX KEYS

A hex key is a screwdriver with a six-sided tip. Hex keys are also called Allen wrenches.

different sizes of hex keys

Six-sided shapes are called hexagons.

set of hex keys attached to a ring

Hex keys turn screws with six-sided **sockets.**

the head of a socket-head screw

The hex key fits **snugly** in the socket. Hex keys are small, light, and easy to manufacture.

folding hex-key set

Ellen is putting together a bookshelf.
She tightens a screw with a hex key.

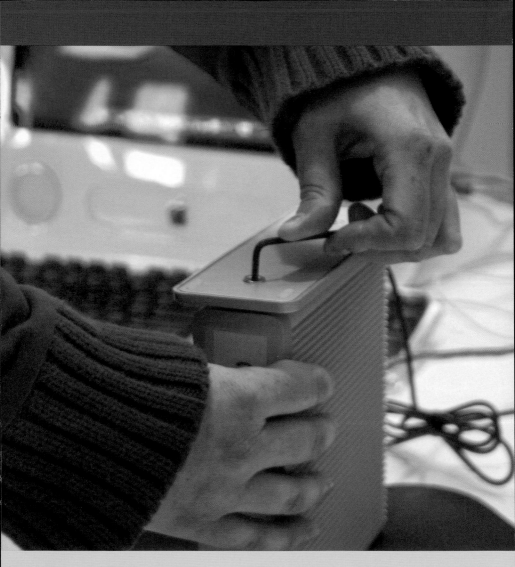

Shelby is fixing a computer part. She removes a **socket**-head screw with a hex key.

MATCH GAME

Match the words to the pictures! The answers are on the bottom of the page.

1. Phillips screwdriver

A.

2. screw gun

B.

3. slotted screwdriver

C.

4. hex keys

D.

TOOL QUIZ

Test your tool knowledge with this quiz!
The answers are on the bottom of the page.

1. The first screwdrivers were slotted screwdrivers.
   True or false?

2. Phillips screwdrivers turn slotted screws. True or false?

3. Some screw guns use strips of screws. True or false?

4. A hex key has a seven-sided tip. True or false?

GLOSSARY

attach – to secure or join.

drive – to use physical force to make something move.

fasten – to attach something.

friction – the resistance between two surfaces that are touching each other.

install – to set up something and get it ready to use.

repair – to fix something.

slot – narrow opening or groove.

snug – very tight or close-fitting.

socket – an opening that holds something, such as a light socket.

To see a complete list of SandCastle™ books and other nonfiction titles from ABDO Publishing Company, visit www.abdopublishing.com.

8000 West 78th Street, Edina, MN 55439 • 800-800-1312 • fax 952-831-1632